The Ultimate Keyb
CHORD CHAR

MW01003008

Introduction

The *Ultimate Keyboard Chord Chart* has been created to assist you in learning to play today s most commonly used chords. It is a fast and fun way to gain instant access to 120 essential voicings: just look up a chord and you can easily find out how to play it.

This book will not only show you the different chords and their locations, but will provide the fundamentals behind how and why each chord is constructed. This approach to learning will greatly enhance your playing and understanding of the material introduced.

How to Use this Book

To use the chart on the following pages, simply find the *letter name* of the chord along the top of the chart, and the *kind of chord* (major, minor, etc.) in the column at the left. Read across and down to find the correct chord.

Each chord is playable by the right hand, and is positioned near middle C on the keyboard:

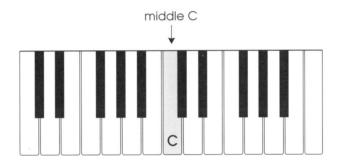

HAL•LEONARD®
CORPORATION

7777 W. BLUEMOUND RD. P.O. BOX 13819 MILWAUKEE, WI 53213

Visit Hal Leonard online at
www.halleonard.com

	C	Dᵇ(C#)

	C	**D♭ (C♯)**
MAJOR	G C E	A♭ D♭ F
MINOR (M)	G C E♭	A♭ D♭ F♭
AUGMENTED (+)	C E G♯	A D♭ F
SUSPENDED FOURTH (SUS4)	G C F	A♭ D♭ G♭
SIXTH (6)	G A C E	A♭ B♭ D♭ F
SEVENTH (7)	G B♭ C E	A♭ C♭ D♭ F
MAJOR SEVENTH (MAJ7)	G B E	A♭ C F
MINOR SEVENTH (M7)	G B♭ C E♭	A♭ C♭ D♭ F♭
DIMINISHED SEVENTH (°7)	G♭ B♭♭ C E♭	A♭♭ B♭ D♭ F♭
NINTH (9)	G B♭ D E	A♭ C♭ E♭ F

	D	E♭
MAJOR	F♯ A D	B♭ E♭ G
MINOR (M)	A D F	G♭ B♭ E♭
AUGMENTED (+)	F♯ A♯ D	G B E♭
SUSPENDED FOURTH (SUS4)	G A D	A♭ B♭ E♭
SIXTH (6)	F♯ A B D	G B♭ C E♭
SEVENTH (7)	F♯ A C D	G B♭ D♭ E♭
MAJOR SEVENTH (MAJ7)	F♯ A C♯	G B♭ D
MINOR SEVENTH (M7)	A C D F	G♭ B♭ D♭ E♭
DIMINISHED SEVENTH (°7)	A♭ C♭ D F	G♭ B♭♭ D♭♭ E♭
NINTH (9)	F♯ A C E	G B♭ D♭ F

	E	F
MAJOR	G#, B, E	A, C, F
MINOR (M)	G, B, E	A♭, C, F
AUGMENTED (+)	G#, B#, E	C#, A, F
SUSPENDED FOURTH (SUS4)	A, B, E	B♭, C, F
SIXTH (6)	G#, C#, B, E	A, C, D, F
SEVENTH (7)	G#, B, D, E	E♭, A, C, F
MAJOR SEVENTH (MAJ7)	G#, D#, B	A, C, E
MINOR SEVENTH (M7)	G, B, D, E	A♭, E♭, C, F
DIMINISHED SEVENTH (°7)	B♭, D♭, G, E	A♭, C♭, E♭♭, F
NINTH (9)	G#, F#, B, D	E♭, A, C, G

	F♯(G♭)	G
MAJOR	F♯, A♯, C♯	G, B, D
MINOR (M)	F♯, A, C♯	G, B♭, D
AUGMENTED (+)	F♯, A♯, D	G, B, D♯
SUSPENDED FOURTH (SUS4)	F♯, B, C♯	G, C, D
SIXTH (6)	F♯, A♯, C♯, D♯	G, B, D, E
SEVENTH (7)	F♯, A♯, C♯, E	G, B, D, F
MAJOR SEVENTH (MAJ7)	A♯, C♯, E♯	F♯, B, D
MINOR SEVENTH (M7)	F♯, A, C♯, E	G, B♭, D, F
DIMINISHED SEVENTH (°7)	F♯, A, C, E♭	G, B♭, D♭, F♭
NINTH (9)	G♯, A♯, C♯, E	A, B, D, F

	A♭ (G♯)	A
MAJOR	A♭, C, E♭	C♯, A, E
MINOR (M)	A♭, C♭, E♭	A, C, E
AUGMENTED (+)	A♭, C, E	C♯, A, E♯
SUSPENDED FOURTH (SUS4)	A♭, D♭, E♭	A, D, E
SIXTH (6)	A♭, C, E♭, F	F♯, A, C♯, E
SEVENTH (7)	G♭, A♭, C, E♭	C♯, G, A, E
MAJOR SEVENTH (MAJ7)	G, C, E♭	G♯, C♯, E
MINOR SEVENTH (M7)	G♭, A♭, C♭, E♭	G, A, C, E
DIMINISHED SEVENTH (°7)	A♭, C♭, E♭♭, G♭♭	G♭, A, C, E♭
NINTH (9)	G♭, B♭, C, E♭ (G♯)	C♯, G, B, E

	B♭	B
MAJOR	B♭, D, F	F♯, D♯, B
MINOR (M)	B♭, D♭, F	F♯, B, D
AUGMENTED (+)	F♯, B♭, D	D♯, G, B
SUSPENDED FOURTH (SUS4)	B♭, E♭, F	F♯, B, E
SIXTH (6)	G, B♭, D, F	F♯, G♯, D♯, B
SEVENTH (7)	A♭, B♭, D, F	F♯, D♯, A, B
MAJOR SEVENTH (MAJ7)	F, A, D	F♯, A♯, D♯
MINOR SEVENTH (M7)	A♭, B♭, D♭, F	F♯, A, B, D
DIMINISHED SEVENTH (°7)	A♭♭, B♭, D♭, F♭	A♭, B, D, F
NINTH (9)	A♭, B♭, C, D, F	F♯, A, C♯, D♯

ABOUT CHORDS

What Is a Chord?

A chord is defined as three or more notes played at the same time. Chords provide the *harmony* that supports the melody of a song.

Sometimes chords are indicated by *chord symbols*, written above the musical staff. A chord symbol is simply an abbreviation for the name of that chord. For example, the symbol for an *F-sharp minor seven* chord would be F#m7.

How Are Chords Formed?

Chords are constructed from a combination of various scale steps. Major scales are constructed by a series of whole steps and half steps. Each step is numbered:

C MAJOR SCALE

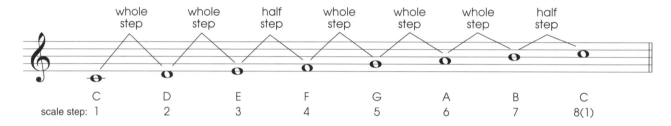

These same numbers are used to indicate which steps of a scale must be combined to form the chord. The chart below is a construction summary of the chord types in this book (based on the key of C only). Use the numeric formula given to determine which tones from the major scale are contained in a certain chord. For example, based on the C major scale, 1-♭3-5 would mean play the root (C), a flatted third (E♭), and the fifth (G)—a C minor chord.

CHORD TYPE	FORMULA	NOTE NAMES	CHORD NAMES
major	1-3-5	C-E-G	C
minor	1-♭3-5	C-E♭-G	Cm
augmented	1-3-#5	C-E-G#	C+
suspended fourth	1-4-5	C-F-G	Csus4
sixth	1-3-5-6	C-E-G-A	C6
seventh	1-3-5-♭7	C-E-G-B♭	C7
major seventh	1-3-5-7	C-E-G-B	Cmaj7
minor seventh	1-♭3-5-♭7	C-E♭-G-B♭	Cm7
diminished seventh	1-♭3-♭5-♭♭7	C-E♭-G♭-B♭♭	C°7
ninth	1-3-5-♭7-9	C-E-G-B♭-D	C9

Now, this is how chords are built *in theory*. But it's not necessarily how chords are *played*. These notes can be arranged in different positions on the fretboard, like this:

C MAJOR

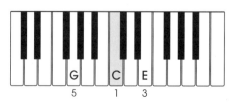